THE
ADRIAN MOLE
DIARY
1986

TWO-CAN DESIGN

First published in 1985 by
Two-Can Design Ltd
71 Fanshaw Street
London N1
01-729 4000

Edited by Claudia Zeff
Handwriting by Greg Ward
Typeset in Bembo by Chestnut Phototypesetting Ltd, Wembley
Origination by Apple Graphics
Printed in Great Britain

ISBN 0 413 59860 8

THIS BOOK
BELONGS TO

Adrian Mole

JANUARY

Thursday 2

Friday 3

When I got up this morning I vowed to do something out of
the ordinary. I started my unusual life by washing behind
my ears. Then I parted my hair in a different way. My
parents didn't notice. They were too busy bickering over
the electricity bill even to give me a second look.

Saturday 4

Sunday 5

Instead of calling for Pandora like I usually do. I
went for a walk along the canal bank. I spent a most
enjoyable hour there throwing stones at an old pram that
a litter lout had thrown into the water.

RESOLUTIONS

1. I will try not to use so many exclamation marks.
2. I will stop telling my mother that her hair is going grey.
3. I will stop telling my father that his hair is falling out.
4. I will be kind to people, animals and insects.
5. I will stop looking in the mirror 500 times a day.
6. I will forbid Pandora to smoke her stinking fags in my bedroom.
7. I _will_ be dead rich and dead famous before I am 25
8. I will cut down on my drinking (½ lager a week)
9. I will stop talking about the Norwegian Leather Industry.
10. I will never vote Conservative.

JANUARY

Monday 6
EPIPHANY

Tuesday 7

Wednesday 8

Thursday 9
Mr and Mrs Singh have invited me and Pandora to their
daughter's wedding. It is a Sikh wedding so I asked
Mr Singh if I would be expected to wear a turban.

Friday 10

Saturday 11

English weddings are dead boring compared to Sikh ones.
We all had a brilliant time; nobody told us to be quiet
or minded that we couldn't sing the hymns.

Sunday 12

Stayed in bed all day recovering from the wedding.
Mr Singh and his relations are still celebrating.
I don't know how they do it.

JANUARY

Monday 13

I have had a note from Mrs Singh's daughter. 'Thank you
very much for your present. I have always wanted a
wooden ash tray.' What cheek! It took me all of ten
weeks of woodwork lessons to carve that bread board!

Tuesday 14

My mother has been comforting Mrs Singh. She is dead upset
at losing her daughter. Apparently after we all left the
reception a row broke out between the two families. So it
has been an English wedding after all.

Wednesday 15

Thursday 16

JANUARY

Friday 17

Pandora has been elected Form Captain. We had a secret
ballot. There are 29 in our form. She got 28 votes and
I got one. I voted for myself. I hope she doesn't find
out.

Saturday 18

Sunday 19

JANUARY

Monday 20
MARTIN LUTHER KING DAY (USA)

Felt sad.

Tuesday 21
I'm getting dead worried about my GCE work. I am sure
to fail my exams. My problem is I am too intellectual.
I am always thinking things like: is there a God? And:
where do flies go in the winter?

Wednesday 22
Pandora is dead lucky: her brain is straight-forward so
she can remember the names of all Henry VIII's wives.
In order!

Thursday 23

Friday 24

I keep telling my mother that our dog's behaviour is
abnormal and I am always asking her to take it for
special Barbara Woodhouse training but she refuses.
I know why. It is because she is scared of being told
off by Barbara Woodhouse. My mother spoilt the dog rotten
when it was a pup, and now the whole family is suffering
because of it.

Saturday 25

Sunday 26

I did body-building exercises for most of the day. I
measured my muscles this evening, but there was no
improvement.

JANUARY

Monday 27

Tuesday 28

Pandora has reassured me that she likes skinny boys. She
says that they have a greater depth, but it's not depth
I'm worried about, it's width.

Wednesday 29

ADRIAN MOLE
loves
Pandora

JANUARY

Thursday 30

We have got a dead good new bathroom carpet. It is
100 per cent acrylic shagpile. It is the height of
taste and luxury. I feel like Omar Sharif when I am
standing on it with my naked feet.

Friday 31

School was good today. My English essay 'Despair' got
twenty out of twenty and was read out to the class.
Everyone looked dead miserable at the end. Pandora's
eyes were full of tears. I think I would like to be
a full time writer, it must be a dead cushy job just
sitting around writing essays.

Saturday 1

Sunday 2

FEBRUARY

Monday 3

Tuesday 4

Wednesday 5

Thursday 6

Barry Kent has been suspended from school for writing on
the toilet walls. He wrote: 'Why is there never any
toilet paper in here?'

FEBRUARY

Friday 7

Some more graffiti appeared on the toilet walls today.
It said: 'Barry Kent is innocent.' It was written very
nicely in blue felt tip pen during morning break. I know
because I wrote it!

Barry Kent is inner Barry Kent is inners Barry Kent is Barry Ken is innocent

Saturday 8

Saw Barry Kent and
his gang messing
about outside the Chinese chip shop. Barry made an
inarticulate speech about how I would make a good
member of his gang. I tried to decline gracefully, but
Barry Kent isn't the sort of boy you can say no to.

Sunday 9

A sleepless night worrying about Barry Kent's invitation.
I have sent Barry Kent the following note. 'Dear Baz.
Thanks for the honour of being invited to join your gang, but
I must graciously decline. I cannot spare the time from my
studies. Yours respectfully, 'Brains' Mole.'

FEBRUARY

Monday 10
I have wiped my graffiti off the toilet walls.

Tuesday 11
SHROVE TUESDAY

Ate 19 pancakes. Only stopped because I ran out of lemons.

Wednesday 12
ASH WEDNESDAY

Thursday 13
Nigel's parents are going to London for the weekend so Nigel is throwing a party for 50 close friends. All guests must dress in black from head to toe.

FEBRUARY

Friday 14
VALENTINE'S DAY

I asked my mother to buy me a pair of black jeans, a black
grandad shirt, a black leather tie, a black vest, black
underpants and black socks. But she refused. I have never
known such a stingey woman.

Saturday 15
Bought black dye for mixed fibres, put white shirt,
burgundy cords, red socks and blue underwear in washing
machine. Painted white training shoes with black gloss
paint. Went back to washing machine to find everything
a yukky grey.

Sunday 16
The party was dead disappointing; it finished at 9.30
when a woman over the road told the police that black-
clothed devil worshippers had broken into Nigel's house.

FEBRUARY

Monday 17

Nigel's parents have locked him in the house. He is not allowed out until the black footprints have been removed from the lounge carpet.

Tuesday 18

Wednesday 19

Pandora has got three spots on her face! She sent me a note saying that she would be off school until they had cleared up. Poor Pandora, I know how she feels, but if I stayed off school every time a new spot appeared on my face I would never have a mark in the register.

Thursday 20

I rang Pandora to ask how her spots were. She said tearfully, 'I've got five today.' I tried to cheer her up by saying, 'That's nothing, I've got fifteen!'

FEBRUARY

Friday 21

Saturday 22

I've swallowed a grape pip. Now I could get appendicitis.

Sunday 23

In bed with stomach ache waiting for my appendix to
rupture.

FEBRUARY

Monday 24
FULL MOON

DOG WENT BARMY

Tuesday 25
This morning my Mother said, 'There is no way I'm going
to spend the rest of my life in this dump!' She wants
to live in the boring COUNTRY! She wants a wrecked-up
cottage. And to keep goats.

Wednesday 26
My mother came back from the library with 'Goatkeeping -
An Introduction' and a bird-spotting book. She stayed
in the garden till dark staring at birds. Our tea was
very late.

Thursday 27

FEBRUARY

Friday 28

Saturday 1

It is Grandma's birthday today. I bought her a card and
a £1 book token. I wanted the dog to sign it so I
rubbed the dog's paw with black felt-tipped pen and then
pressed its paw inside the card.

Sunday 2

I will be sixteen in one month's time.

MARCH

Monday 3

Tuesday 4

We did "The Skin" today in biology. Mr Brunel the
teacher drew a diagram of a big skin pore on the
blackboard. It was revolting, full of gooey stuff.
At break time nobody felt like eating their crisps.

Wednesday 5

MARCH

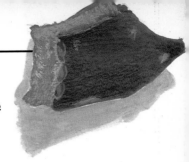

Thursday 6
Domestic science was brilliant today.
We cooked chocolate. (I ate every piece
on my way home.)

Friday 7

Saturday 8
Pandora and I had a good talk about life today.   We
both agreed that on the whole it is better than death
so at last we agree on something.

Sunday 9
MOTHERING SUNDAY

Paid two quid
for scabby plant

MARCH

Monday 10

I walked to boring school. The row and chaos on the
bus are too much for my nerves.

Tuesday 11

Wednesday 12

For once a smashing day at school. Several new
dinner monitors were announced in Assembly and Pandora
is one of them. She gave me three helpings of chips, so
I know she still loves me.

Thursday 13

Friday 14

Saturday 15

Did my own washing this morning because I'm fed up with wearing pink underpants and vests. My father is in charge of doing the washing but he always puts his red handkerchiefs in with the whites.

Sunday 16

BRITISH SUMMER TIME BEGINS

Rained All Day

MARCH

Monday 17
ST PATRICK'S DAY (BANK HOLIDAY IN NORTHERN IRELAND)

Tuesday 18

Wednesday 19
Did my chemistry homework on the bus going to school.
I think it's disgusting that Britain's roads are in
such a state. Potholes and lumps in the road make my
handwriting terrible.

Thursday 20

MARCH

Friday 21

Saturday 22

Went to see 'E T' for the seventh time. As usual
Pandora cried on the bus going home but I waited
until I got into my bedroom.

Sunday 23
PALM SUNDAY

My mother has gone
out for the day with
her women's group.
My father and me had
tomato soup for Sunday
dinner and a Mars bar
and tin of beans for
Sunday tea. It was dead
good. Hardly any washing
up!

MARCH

Monday 24
During geography I looked out of the window and saw what I
thought was a condor flying over the school playground.
However, Mr Baldrey, the geography teacher, said it was more
likely to be a crow. Just my luck.

Tuesday 25
Woke up with a tongue ache. I've never heard of anyone
suffering from tongue ache before. Perhaps I will make
medical history. My mother advised me not to talk to
anyone, especially her. Had day off school. Ha! Ha! Ha!

Wednesday 26
FULL MOON
Tongue ache a bit better.

Dog went berserk

Thursday 27
Tongue completely better.

MARCH

Friday 28
GOOD FRIDAY

Saturday 29
Tonight I saw a programme on the cruelties of whale
hunting. I told my mother she ought to throw all her
lipsticks and perfumes away, because parts of whales are
used in their manufacture. Must stop now - the phone is
ringing. I expect it's Pandora planning our next
campaign.

Sunday 30
EASTER DAY
Had Grandma for tea. (We didn't eat her she just came.
Ha! Ha!). The dog stole a bakewell tart. That only left
three so guess who had to go without.

got pathetic small egg !!!

MARCH

Monday 31
BANK HOLIDAY IN UK (EXCEPT SCOTLAND)

No money as usual.

Tuesday 1
ALL FOOL'S DAY

For a joke, told my father he'd won the pools. He hit me later.

Wednesday 2
Pandora has bought a pair of pink leather boots with very high heels, thus forcing me to walk on tip-toe. I prefer her to wear track shoes, it's the only time we see eye-to-eye.

Thursday 3
Pandora is beside herself with grief and despair. She caught a heel of her new boots in a grating and pulled it off. Ha! Ha! Ha!

APRIL

Friday 4

I woke up with a brilliant feeling
inside me today. Feeling really inspired,
I started to write a poem before I ate my
cornflakes.
I didn't finish it because my mum is a Philistine and
wanted to clear the breakfast table. I bet William
Wordsworth's mother didn't nag him when he was writing
his daffodil poem.

Saturday 5

Sunday 6

APRIL

Monday 7

Did brilliant history essay. I wrote about the
exploitation of child labour in the nineteenth century.
Nothing has changed. My parents would send me up a
chimney if we had a chimney.

Tuesday 8

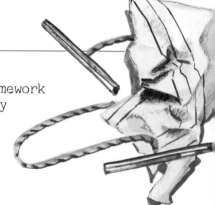

Wednesday 9

The dog has chewed my history homework
folder. I told Mr Fillingham, my
history teacher, but he accused
me of telling lies. I offered
to be strapped to a lie
detector.

APRIL

Thursday 10

Did history homework again. Locked the dog in the coal
shed just to be on the safe side.

Friday 11

Saturday 12

Got up and left the house early, so avoided doing my
homework. Went for a bike ride and tried to find some
countryside but it was behind barbed wire, so I came
home and had dinner.

Sunday 13

APRIL

Monday 14

Oh joy!... Oh rapture! At last I have made
my mark on the world of literature. My essay
entitled 'A day in the life of an Air
Stewardess' has won second prize in the
inter-comprehensive schools fifth year
creative writing competition. My prizes
are: A Concorde-shaped bookmark enscribed
by Melvyn Bragg and an all expenses
trip to Leningrad.

Concorde

Tuesday 15

Wednesday 16

My family has been in a blind panic ever since the
telemessage arrived. None of us know how to get hold
of a passport.

APRIL

Thursday 17

Pandora said I could get a passport from the head office in Peterborough.

Friday 18

Mrs Braithwaite, Pandora's mother, took me to Peterborough on the back of her motorbike. For a Marriage Guidance Counsellor she certainly knows how to burn the road up.

Saturday 19

Sunday 20

APRIL

Monday 21

My father has been trying to ring the Russian Embassy all
day to enquire about a visa. So far he has had no luck.
A bloke shouts 'Niet!!' in a growly voice and slams the
phone down.

Tuesday 22

I rang Bert Baxter and asked his advice on how to get a
visa. Bert said 'Visa?...You're too young to have a
credit card ain't you?'

Wednesday 23
ST GEORGE'S DAY

Happy Birthday. Signed - A. Dragon.

Thursday 24

After school I went to the travel agents to enquire about
a visa. A fair-haired girl with a heavy cold said I would
have to go to London and take my passport and three
photographs to the 'Intourist' office. Tonight before
bed I made my mother write a note to school.

APRIL

Friday 25
London!...
The Celestial
City!

Dear Mrs Fossington-Gore

Adrian is unable to come to school on Monday because he has urgent business to attend in London.

Yours faithfully
Ms. Pauline Mole

Saturday 26

Sunday 27

APRIL

Monday 28

I felt dead scared when I got off the train at
St Pancras. Somehow I had to get to Regent Street with
only my father's AA map of London. When I finally got to
the Intourist office a cockney girl behind the counter
asked me ten questions, only one of which I could
answer (Date of Birth). Then she said that my visa would
be sent to me automatically. I said that my travel agent
had told me otherwise. She said 'You should change your
travel agent, sonny'.

Tuesday 29

I sincerely hope my father has got an AA book for
Moscow and Leningrad, for without it I am lost.

Wednesday 30

Thursday 1

Friday 2

Saturday 3

I lay awake for hours last night worrying about Moscow
and Leningrad. Would the Russians stare at my pointed
head and make mocking remarks in Russian?

Sunday 4

MAY

Monday 5
BANK HOLIDAY

Tuesday 6
For the past week my sleep has been invaded by nightmares
about Russia. In my dreams Mr Gorbachov meets me at
Moscow Airport dressed in a bear suit. He is holding a
hammer and sickle in his paws.

Wednesday 7
ASCENSION DAY
2 a.m. just woken up to have another worry about the
non-appearance of my visa.
4 a.m. woke up again to have another visa worry, so
that's one thousand, nine hundred and twenty-three
worries today... I can't take much more.
Got up at 6.30 worried about visa. Attended to my
toilet. Ironed my third-best trousers and my fourth-
best shirt. Thus fortified I sat on the stairs and
waited for Courtney Elliot to arrive with the post.
At 7.30 I got bored, so I started to read 'The Guardian'.
A headline immediately caught my eye: 'MOLE UNCOVERED
IN MOSCOW'.

MAY

Thursday 8

Friday 9   DAY OF DEPARTURE

6.30 got up, checked spots in wardrobe mirror.
Got dressed in second-best clothes, checked suitcase,
tied labels on, checked medical supplies (junior aspirins
in case I get one of my headaches).
7.35 will Courtney Elliot have my visa?
4 p.m. I am writing this on the plane. I couldn't
write before because my hands wouldn't stop trembling.
5.45 we have landed.

Saturday 10

Sunday 11

It's brilliant in Russia. They eat cakes for breakfast.
However I was amazed that a hotel such as the Cosmos
could run out of milk...
4.30 I am going to the hotel dinner dance tonight.
Apparently dinner jackets are seen by the Russians as the
ultimate Bourgeois symbol. No wonder I was hissed as I
drank my Beetroot soup.

MAY

Monday 12

Went to Red Square and the Kremlin today. St Basil's
Cathedral is a bit over the top in my opinion, it looks
as if a lunatic was let loose with a paintbrush.

Tuesday 13

I went to the Museum of Russian Folk Art today. Saw it.
Came back. Went to the Opera at eight...I fell asleep.

Wednesday 14

Thursday 15

LENINGRAD

2.30 p.m. Just got back from a coach tour of Leningrad.
It is a brilliant city; statues and monuments and museums
and culture galore.

MAY

Friday 16
PUSHKIN

Pushkin is where
Catherine The Great
ordered thousands
of serfs to build her
a Summer Palace.
They did a good job.
4.30 p.m. HERMITAGE
Such a surfeit of
art and beauty in
one day is just too
much.

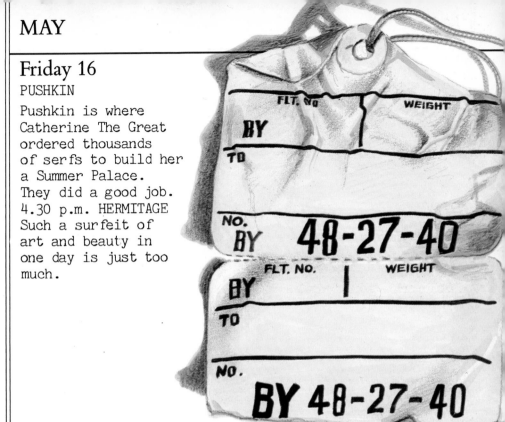

Saturday 17
We saw groups of Russian people sunbathing against a wall.
They had the forethought to put rouble notes over their
noses as a guard against sunburned conks.

Sunday 18
WHIT SUNDAY

Grabbed two sets of Russian dolls from the souvenir
shop in the hotel. They are dead good value, because
within the largest doll nest eight more, so I will split
them up and give the people at home <u>one</u> each. Ha! Ha! Ha!

MAY

Monday 19

Hegel, Lenin's favourite philosopher, said life proceeds
by contradictions and I, Adrian Mole, aged nearly
seventeen, am inclined to agree.

Tuesday 20

Wednesday 21

The sight of English consumers feverishly buying goods
in the shops has sent me mad with culture shock.

MAY

Thursday 22

Found my mother staring into the mirror counting her wrinkles;
she said she has got 18 but I could only see nine. However,
I pointed out to my mother that she has got loads of grey
hairs, and for some reason she went mad.

Friday 23
FULL MOON

Dog beside itself.
Mad as march hare.

Saturday 24

Sunday 25
TRINITY SUNDAY

MAY

Monday 26
SPRING BANK HOLIDAY

Tuesday 27

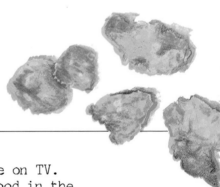

Wednesday 28
I have just watched a programme on TV.
It was all about the lack of food in the
Third World. Then there was an advertisement showing
cream cakes. I went to bed without eating my usual
digestive biscuits.

MAY

Thursday 29

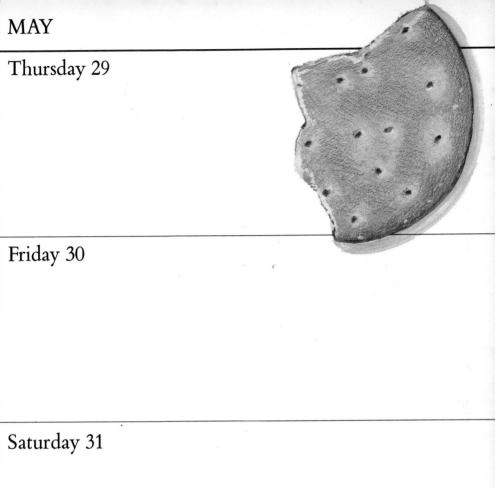

Friday 30

Saturday 31

Sunday 1

Stayed in bed till 1.30 p.m.. so missed breakfast.
I asked my mother to donate the cost of my breakfast to
the Oxfam fund, but she refused.

JUNE

Monday 2

Tuesday 3
Bought my first Mars Bar for five days. It was
delicious, and I only felt a bit guilty eating it.

Wednesday 4
Went to the barber's today. I asked for a 'flick-
head' (the latest style). Pandora has agreed to go
on seeing me but only on condition I wear a hat at
all times. Grandma thinks my hair looks dead good.
She says it reminds her of the War.

Thursday 5
Brillo pad news! Nigel has copied my hair style. He
is the fashion leader at school so at last I can discard
my wooly hat. Apparently the style is called 'The
Ration Book'.

JUNE

Friday 6

Saturday 7

Pandora and I went to Marks & Spencer and bought some half- English half-French micro pants. I look dead virile and sexy in them. It's a pity that nobody is going to see them.

Sunday 8

JUNE

Monday 9

Tuesday 10

Wednesday 11

Thursday 12

I have taken up bird-watching, partly because it is a
way of getting some fresh air and partly because I read
somewhere that it is good for the nerves.

JUNE

Friday 13

<u>8 p.m.</u> I saw 89 birds. I don't know what type they were
because I haven't got a decent reference book yet.
The children's encyclopedia is too big and heavy to lug
about all day.

Saturday 14

I found a dead good bird book called 'The Observer's Book
of Birds' for £2.50. It just fits into the pocket of my
anorak.

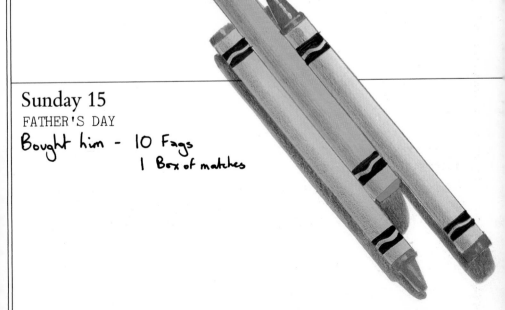

Sunday 15

FATHER'S DAY

Bought him - 10 Fags
            1 Box of matches

JUNE

Monday 16

Tuesday 17

Wednesday 18

I am sick of not getting enough attention. My mother
spends all her time fussing over the stupid pot plants.
She talks to them in a much kinder voice than she uses
to me.

Thursday 19

JUNE

Friday 20
People for miles around have heard about my mother's
skills and have started bringing dying plants to her.
She has set up a plant recovery room in the corner of
the kitchen.

Saturday 21
Pandora allowed me into her room to listen to her
Flying Pickets record this afternoon. It was like a jungle
in there. Through the greenery I tried to tell her I loved
her but she was too busy repotting a Parlour Palm to listen.

Sunday 22
Went to Grandma's for Sunday tea. She gave me loads of
attention.

JUNE

Monday 23

Tuesday 24

I have started a captive collection of plants on my
bedroom window sill. It's the only way I know of
getting my mother's attention. She spoke to me for
half-an-hour tonight.

Wednesday 25

Thursday 26

I am going on a camping trip with the Youth Club tomorrow
so I have spent all night washing and ironing.

JUNE

Friday 27

Up at 5 a.m. to make a packed lunch for the journey. I
woke my parents at 5.30 a.m. to ask if there was a jar
of crab paste for my sandwiches. Their response was
very unhelpful. Why can't they be more like the parents
in the cornflake advertisement?

Saturday 28

I am writing this in a muddy desolate field somewhere in
Derbyshire. We set up camp last night, but the wind
blew it down this morning.

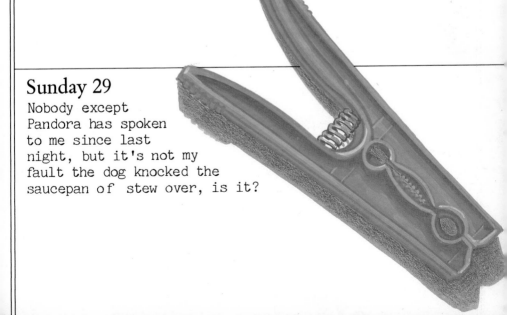

Sunday 29

Nobody except
Pandora has spoken
to me since last
night, but it's not my
fault the dog knocked the
saucepan of stew over, is it?

JUNE

Monday 30
Morale is low. It wasn't my fault it rained and the
camp fire went out, but as usual I'm getting the blame.

Tuesday 1
Only one more day of this ordeal to go. I long for clean
sheets and my electric toothbrush.

Wednesday 2
At last I am back in civilisation. I told my proud
parents that I have been trekking over wild countryside
and climbing sheer rock faces.

JULY

Thursday 3

Got a phone call from a distraught Grandma this morning.
She said: 'Come round quickly, Adrian, something terrible
has happened to my lovely garden.'

Friday 4

AMERICAN INDEPENDENCE DAY

Grandma's garden is no more. Talk about a waste land.
The gnomes stand amongst dead plants grinning stupidly.

Saturday 5

The man from the garden centre called round this
morning with the results of the soil test. He asked
who had watered the garden last. It was a nasty
moment for me. I said I had and I confessed to
adding fertiliser to the watering can. Grandma said:
'You idiot boy, do you think a fertiliser would be
called Killitoff?'

Sunday 6

JULY

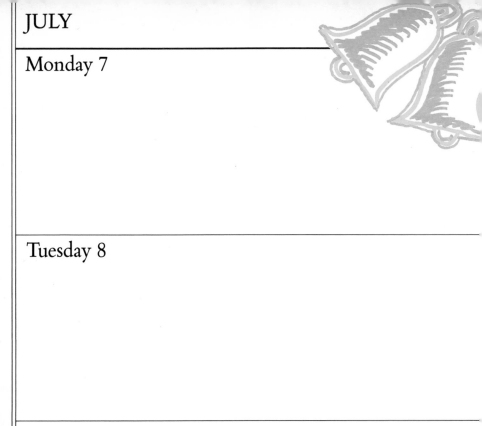

Monday 7

Tuesday 8

Wednesday 9

Thursday 10

I asked Pandora to marry me this morning. We were
leaning over the frozen food cabinet at the time.

JULY

Friday 11
Tonight I asked Pandora if she wanted to get engaged to
me. Pandora said, 'No, thank you - in fact I'm fed up
with going out with you'.

Saturday 12
Pandora asked me not to stand outside her house and
stare up at her window after dark. She said it
gave her the creeps.

Sunday 13

JULY

Monday 14

I didn't call for Pandora on the way to school or sit next to her at school dinner, but I can't say she noticed.

Tuesday 15

I was watching Crossroads when Pandora telephoned and asked to speak to me. I instructed my mother to tell Pandora that I was out at a wild disco.

Wednesday 16

We are together again but there are conditions. I am not allowed to mention marriage or getting engaged or write Mrs Pandora Mole on the inside of my geography book.

Thursday 17

JULY

Friday 18

I asked my mother for advice. She said, 'Adrian, why
can't you just be fond of Pandora? Why do you have to
dramatise everything in your life?' She can talk -
when she burns the toast she acts as if it was a scene
from The Towering Inferno.

Saturday 19

Sunday 20

Mr and Mrs. A. Mole

Mr and Mrs Adrian Mole

Mr and Mrs A. Mole

Pandora Mole

P. Mole.

JULY

Monday 21
FULL MOON

Dog HOOOWLING up at night sky

Tuesday 22

Wednesday 23

Thursday 24
My mother has pulled a muscle in her back. Dr Gray came
and said she must lie flat on the floor for a week. She
chose to be on the sitting room floor, which is most
inconvenient.

JULY

Friday 25

The window cleaner came just before I left for rotten
school. He shouted through the sitting room window:
'Drunk again, Mrs Mole?'

Saturday 26

I am worn out with fetching things for my mother.
I'll be glad when her muscle is unpulled.

Sunday 27

JULY

Monday 28

Dr Gray called today and told my mother to lie on a
door! How stupid can you get?

Tuesday 29

Wednesday 30

My mother's back is completely better but she is
still not doing any housework.

Thursday 31

Pandora is back from her Portuguese villa holiday.
She bought me a stuffed donkey and a straw hat back.
She confessed she had fallen in love with a bloke
called Pedro. He is dead rich.

AUGUST

Friday 1
The horrible Pedro phoned Pandora last night.

Saturday 2
I told my mother about Pandora's new love and she said
that Pedro was probably a waiter.

Sunday 3
I rang the hotel and asked for Pedro. A foreign voice
said 'we ave two Pedros 'ere, one is a kitchen porter
and the other is cleaning out the hotel swimming pool'.
I said 'Aha!' and put the phone down.

Portugal

01 0~~34~~ Spain

5211320 Si

AUGUST

Monday 4

I told Pandora the
truth about Pedro.
To my astonishment she
accused me of being
sneaky and
underhand.

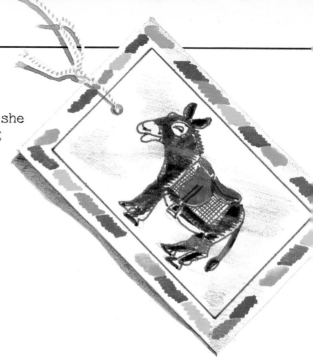

Tuesday 5

Pandora received a postcard from Pedro today. He
said he was coming to visit her and would be staying
for three months.

Wednesday 6

Pandora's holiday romance is over. She said she
wanted to remember Pedro as she last saw him with
his handsome face bathed in a Portuguese sunset.

AUGUST

Thursday 7

I have formed a club for non-smokers at school. It's called Stub it out, or SIT for short. Pandora is not in it because she smokes at least three Benson & Hedges a week.

Friday 8

Barry Kent, who smokes at least ten No 6 every day, has just won the school's cross-country race. This has made me realise that there's just no justice in the world.

Saturday 9

Sunday 10

Grandma came for tea and stayed for supper and Ovaltine. She is breaking in a new pair of false teeth, so she didn't say much.

AUGUST

Monday 11

Tuesday 12

Wednesday 13

Thursday 14

I asked my mother what the Family Allowance is spent on
every week. She said, 'Oh, I buy things like Chanel
No 5 with it - necessities like that'. It is supposed
to be spent on buying MY food and socks etc.

AUGUST

Friday 15

I asked my mother if I can have the Family Allowance
money to myself. I said I would buy my own food and
clothes with it.

Saturday 16

Saved money by not eating breakfast.

Sunday 17

I ate bread and jam for breakfast and dinner.

AUGUST

Monday 18
Shopped for food this afternoon. I bought ½ pound
scrag end, 2 carrots, 1 onion and 1 pound of potatoes
and an Oxo cube.

Tuesday 19
I bravely turned down my mother's roast lamb and
warmed up yesterday's scrag end stew.

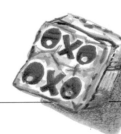

Wednesday 20
I delivered the following note to my mother this
morning: 'I now realise that it is not possible to feed
and clothe myself on £6.50 a week. I hereby give up my
rights to the Family Allowance. Adrian Mole.'

Thursday 21

AUGUST

Friday 22

Saturday 23

I am really fed-up. Everybody is on holiday apart from me. I keep getting postcards from exotic places. Mr & Mrs Singh are in Katmandu, Bert is in Torquay and Barry Kent is in Borstal.

Sunday 24

Moped about the house all day. Washed up twice. Cleaned the bathroom. Sunbathed in the garden until it started to rain.

AUGUST

Monday 25
LATE SUMMER BANK HOLIDAY (UK EXCEPT SCOTLAND)
Stayed in bed all day. Read old Beano annuals.

Tuesday 26

Wednesday 27

Thursday 28
I am writing my diary in my darkened bedroom - a
casualty of sunstroke, prickly heat and sunburn.
This is just my luck!

AUGUST

Friday 29

I am reading Love in a Cold Climate by Nancy Mitford.

Saturday 30

I emerged from my bedroom today to face the boiling
sun. I made sure that every surface of my body was
well covered but my mother made me take my Balaclava
helmet off before I went to buy some more sunburn
lotion.

Sunday 31

SEPTEMBER

Monday 1

The sun has disfigured me. I look like a scabby
peeling lobster with dried out hair. I will be glad
when it rains.

Tuesday 2

We have had salad for the sixth day running.

Wednesday 3

At last! It rained today.

Thursday 4

Pandora has got a magnificent tan due to a very
expensive French tanning lotion. I don't know how she
can even bear to look in my direction.

SEPTEMBER

Friday 5

It's raining again. I walked about in my Wellingtons
feeling happy. I am a true Englishman. Foreigners can
keep their rotten sun.

Saturday 6

Sunday 7

SEPTEMBER

Monday 8

Tuesday 9

Wednesday 10

Autumn. My favourite time of the year. Season of fruit
and being melancholy in mists. Pandora and me went to
the woods to kick the rustling leaves about.

Thursday 11

SEPTEMBER

Friday 12

It's my mother's birthday on Sunday and I've only got
a quid in my money box. I know she needs new knickers
because she is using her old ones as dusters.

Saturday 13

It took ages to find a pair of knickers for 99 pence,
but Woolworth's had some. The cashier said in a loud
sort of voice, 'Did you want these knickers in <u>extra</u>
<u>large</u>?' I was so humiliated that I left the change
on the counter!

Sunday 14

My mother was delighted with my present. She went
straight upstairs and put them on. In the afternoon
we had a birthday tea followed by a small disco.
At 9.30 my mother's birthday knickers fell down and
ended up around her ankles. I shouldn't have bought
extra large - she is dead skinny.

SEPTEMBER

Monday 15

I went to school with a hangover. My father's fault
for making me drink half a glass of wine.

Tuesday 16

Barry Kent has heard that I was in Woolworth's
buying extra large knickers. I am staying off school
until the scandal dies down.

Wednesday 17

Found my mother's extra large knickers in the duster
bag. She will get nothing from me next year.

Thursday 18

FULL MOON

Dog had a fit

SEPTEMBER

Friday 19

Saturday 20

Sunday 21

SEPTEMBER

Monday 22

Tuesday 23

Wednesday 24

Thursday 25

Dear Diary, I'm tired and worn out. The reason for my extreme fatigue is not known. I told my mother that I was too exhausted to wash up tonight, but typically she showed me no sympathy. She said I was bone idle.

SEPTEMBER

Friday 26

Yawned all the way through English. Ms Fossington-
Gore was most unkind and sarcastic. She said, 'Adrian
Mole, I have no wish to see the inside of your mouth.
Kindly keep it shut. If I want to see a cavern, I
will go to Derbyshire.'

Saturday 27

Fell asleep in my cornflakes. My mother said it was
the last time she would bring me breakfast in bed.
It took me half an hour to pick the cornflakes out of
my hair.

Sunday 28

Didn't get out of bed until 6 p.m., so I missed Sunday
breakfast, dinner and tea. Just my luck!

SEPTEMBER

Monday 29

Went to see Dr Gray, but fell asleep in the waiting room so missed my 6 p.m. appointment.

Tuesday 30

At 3 a.m. my father came into my room and caught me reading in bed. He said, 'From now on, reading through the night is strictly forbidden.' I must admit to feeling a bit grateful. At least I can get a good night's sleep!

Wednesday 1

OCTOBER

Thursday 2

Friday 3

Couldn't get out of bed, so didn't go to school today.
Why, oh why doesn't somebody do something to help me?
The evidence seems pretty conclusive to me. I have got
the sleeping sickness.

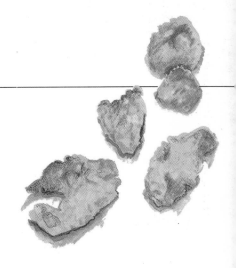

Saturday 4

Sunday 5

OCTOBER

Monday 6

Tuesday 7

Wednesday 8

Thursday 9

```
Pandora is keeping a scrapbook of our romance.  It
is full of strange things.  Tickets of bus journeys we
have shared, a button from my P.E. shorts.  She is
dead romantic.  My ardour for her grows daily.
```

OCTOBER

Friday 10

I suggested to Pandora that we have a night-ritual, that at 10 p.m. wherever we might be we kiss each other's photograph. I gave Pandora a photograph of myself taken at Skegness Pier. It is a brilliant photo. My spots don't show up.

Saturday 11

Forgot to kiss Pandora's picture last night. I'd better not tell her there was an absorbingly brill cowboy film on telly. Pandora went right out of my mind.

Sunday 12

Didn't kiss Pandora's photo because I was in the bath. I am riddled with guilt a bit.

OCTOBER

Monday 13

Saw Pandora on the way to school. She was showing
my photograph to a gang of girls. That photograph
should be a sacred, very private object to her.

Tuesday 14

I avoided Pandora at school. At home time she came up
to me and said. 'Is it all over between us, Aidy?'
I ran off saying I'd got to take Bert to the chiropodist.

Wednesday 15

Thursday 16

Had a full and frank discussion with Pandora during
school dinner. It is 10 o'lock, must stop.

OCTOBER

Friday 17
FULL MOON

DOG AT VETS - SEDATED

Saturday 18

Sunday 19

OCTOBER

Monday 20

Tuesday 21

Wednesday 22

Thursday 23

```
Nigel came round tonight.  He was wearing a new
Italian T-shirt which cost £28!  I asked my parents
for a £28 T-shirt.  They responded by going mad.
```

OCTOBER

Friday 24

I tried to explain to my mother that my standing in
the teenage community would be severely damaged unless
she bought me a £28 T-shirt.

Saturday 25

My mother asked me what this T-shirt looked like. I
told her it had a tiny embroidered crocodile motif
on the breast pocket.

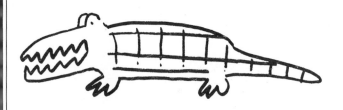

Sunday 26

BRITISH SUMMER TIME ENDS
I want a £28 T-shirt.

Rained All Day

OCTOBER

Monday 27
Had maths test. Got one out of twenty. My mind was
elsewhere, in Italy, where else?

Tuesday 28
Oh joy! Oh rapture! My mother found a crocodile
motif Italian T-shirt in an Oxfam shop for £2. I am
wearing it as I write. Mama mia!

Wednesday 29
Nigel broke the news to me that Italian T-shirts
went out of fashion yesterday. Spanish trousers at
£58.99 are now in vogue.

OCTOBER

Thursday 30

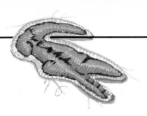

Friday 31

HALLOWEEN

My father bought a gnome with a fishing-rod and put
it in the front garden. My mother objected, but my
father went a bit barmy so she shut up for once.

Saturday 1

Somebody has stolen the gnome's fishing rod! Is
nothing sacred? My father has reported the theft to
the police.

Sunday 2

My parents are not speaking to each other. My father
found the gnome's fishing-rod in my mother's underwear
drawer. It was broken in two. He has informed the police.

NOVEMBER

Monday 3

Tuesday 4

Wednesday 5
```
BONFIRE NIGHT!
```

Thursday 6
```
I have been rehearsing the school play.  It is a free
adaptation of The Cherry Orchard by Anton Chekov.  I am
playing one of the cherry trees in the orchard.
```

NOVEMBER

Friday 7

People don't know how
difficult it is to act
a tree.

Saturday 8

Good news! Barry Kent has dropped out of the play.
I am now playing the leading tree.

Sunday 9

REMEMBRANCE SUNDAY

Got home at 5.39 worn out with standing on my feet
(roots) all day. My tree costume is far too loose.

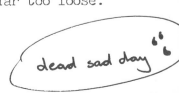

dead sad day

NOVEMBER

Monday 10

Stayed up all night taking in the bark of my trunk.
Must stop the show is about to begin.

Tuesday 11

I can hardly bear to write about last night, but I
must face myself... On second thoughts I just can't
do it. I am a broken man.

Wednesday 12

The following extract from a review of The Cherry
Orchard appeared in the local paper tonight:
'...the cherry tree (lugubriously played by Adrian
Mole) fell...the trunk split open to reveal A Mole
resplendent in his underwear.'

NOVEMBER

Thursday 13

Friday 14

Saturday 15
My mother said if I ever played a tree again she would take the part of a lumberjack.

Sunday 16

NOVEMBER

Monday 17

Tuesday 18

Wednesday 19

Thursday 20
I counted my BBC rejection letters today. So far
I've got seventeen - not bad considering I am only
sixteen. Perhaps I would stand more of a chance if I
typed my poems. I will ask my mother to teach me.

NOVEMBER

Friday 21

Saturday 22

Grandma came round this morning and broke the wonderful
news that she has been elected Editor of the Evergreens
Monthly Newsletter! So, I have a blood relation in a
position of literary influence. I have submitted one
of my best poems, 'Frisky Goats .

Sunday 23

Grandma came to tea. I was especially well-mannered
and attentive. All right, dear Diary, I admit I am
trying to bribe her into accepting 'Frisky Goats' for
publication, but publishing is a cut-throat world
and us poets have to be ruthless sometimes.

NOVEMBER

Monday 24

I am in anguish! The Stupid Evergreens have rejected
'Frisky Goats'. Grandma said, 'We didn't like it
because it doesn't rhyme.'

Tuesday 25

Wednesday 26

Thursday 27

Oh joy! Oh rapture!   The Voice of Youth have published
two of my poems with a smudged photo of myself
looking surly. Underneath the photo it says: 'Adrian
Mole. A future Poet Laureate?'

Friday 28

My mother is thrilled about my poems being published.
She went out and bought two picture frames, pasted
the poems on old postcards, mounted them inside the
frames and then hung them on the wall of the downstairs
lavatory.

Saturday 29

Sunday 30

ST ANDREW'S DAY

Went to have
Sunday dinner at
Grandma's and was
amazed to see my poems
pinned up on her front door.

DECEMBER

Monday 1

The Voice of Youth has sold out and has had to be
reprinted. So I am now a best-selling author!

Tuesday 2

Pandora advised me to stop wearing a floppy bow
round my neck. She pointed out that poets stopped
wearing them a hundred years ago.

Wednesday 3

A very nice man called Brother Ludovic has just called
at the house and spoken to me at great length about
the meaning of life. Brother Ludovic belongs to a
religious society called The Purple People.

DECEMBER

Thursday 4

I am going through a religious experience. Brother
Ludovic said that money, exams and work are evil. He
advised me to give him all my money and not to do my
O levels.

Friday 5

Now my parents have found out about my involvement with
the Purple People. They have decided I can't be trusted
to keep my Building Society savings book in my room.
My father said: 'You'd give your money to every Tom,
Dick or Ludovic who asked for it.'

Saturday 6

Sunday 7

My parents have gone out for the day. I was not invited.
I am feeling a bit hurt about this.

DECEMBER

Monday 8

Tuesday 9

Wednesday 10

Thursday 11

I've been busy training my new pet rat, as yet
unnamed.

DECEMBER

Friday 12

I've decided to call my rat Frank (after Frank Bough). Frank the rat faces a lot of undeserved prejudice from my friends and relations.

Saturday 13

Took Frank for a walk today. The dog sulked because I used his lead.

Sunday 14

Pandora has refused to come into my bedroom when Frank is there, so we didn't have our usual Saturday night kissing session.

DECEMBER

Monday 15

I have written this letter to David Attenborough:
Dear Sir, As a Rat owner I am concerned...

Tuesday 16

Wednesday 17

Took Frank round to Bert Baxter's after school. He
was dead pleased (Bert, not Frank). On the way home
I made enquiries at the pet shop about buying a bat.

DECEMBER

Thursday 18

Friday 19

I had a brilliant letter today. It was from a bloke
called Humphrey Pilkington. He wrote to say that he
had heard I was a poet and he wanted to print a
collection of my latest work! All I have to do is
send him £50! I am going to start saving up.

Saturday 20

Sunday 21

Dear David Attenborou

As a Rat owner I
prejudice by the public to
Can nothing be done to
society. Can you come to
start it? Half-seven woul

Monday 22

Tuesday 23

Wednesday 24

CHRISTMAS EVE

2.15 a.m. Just got back from the Midnight Service.
Once again the Nativity playlet was ruined by having
a live donkey in church. To be fair, the effect of the
Midnight Service was dead moving. Even to me who is a
committed nihilistic existentialist.

Thursday 25

CHRISTMAS DAY

I got the grey zip-up cardigan I asked for (like Frank
Bough's). But the best present was the electric shaver.
I have already had three shaves. Dinner was late as
usual, my mother has never learnt the secret of co-
ordinating the mechanics of a meal. In the evening
we had a desultory game of cards.

DECEMBER

Friday 26
BOXING DAY

Pandora was ecstatic to
see me at first, she
raved about the present
I bought her (a solid
gold bracelet from Tescos,
£2.49) but after a while
she cooled a bit and started
going on about the Christmas house-
party she'd been to. She made a lot of
references to a boy called Crispin
Wartog-Lowndes. I got into a silent jealous
rage. I got into bed at 1 a.m. I am worn out
with all the emotion.

Saturday 27

Sunday 28

DECEMBER

Monday 29

Tuesday 30

My father is growing what's left of his hair. He says it i
the new fashion for men. He says he had hair down to his
shoulders in 1965. I think he's going through the male
menopause.

Wednesday 31

My father got his hippie beads out of the attic last night
If he starts wearing them, I will run away from home.

Thursday 1

NEW YEAR'S DAY

JANUARY

Friday 2

The dog is at the vet's again. It trod in the glue my father
was using to tile the kitchen floor. Its paws got stuck tight
and my father had to cut round the dog with a Stanley knife.
I told the stupid dog to keep still, but would it listen?

Saturday 3

The dog woke me up by jumping on my head. Its mangy tail
got in my mouth (I have been spitting out dog hairs all day).

Sunday 4

ADDRESSES

A

B

BBC Broadcasting House, Portland Place, London.(POEMS)

Simon Bond, 1 Teddy Bear Walk. (Knock three times.
The answer is 'Ready Brek')

Colin Broadway, 10 Lovelorn Avenue, Riverside Park.

C

Carole Hayman, The Joke Shop, 48 Netherhopping Road.

D

Dentist Mr A Grony, 96 Payne Close. Ha! Ha! Ha!
Mr A Bruce, 96 Kangaroo Court, Ha!

ADDRESSES

E

Eddington, the lousy Vet. 2 Barking Road.

Elizabeth (not the Queen) Van Gogh Gardens.

F

Janet Fillingham, Travel Agent, Doughty Street.

G

Giles Gordon, (Community Policeman) 10 Percentage Close.

Glitter (GARY) c/o BBC Centre

H

Caz Holden, (Spike) c/o The Laurels Hostel for Girls,
Penance Lane.

Roger Harris, (Maths Tutor) Charles Street.

Bunny Higginbotham, 99 End Close.

ADDRESSES

I

Irene,Fran,Nancy and Kate. 1, 198 Pollution Park,
Los Angeles, USA Zip code B2192.

J

K

Katrina Wakefield, 91, Royal Court Mews, Acton.

L

Loans and Securities, Unit Two, Starky Avenue.

ADDRESSES

M

Muggy Watson, Borstal, North Sea Camp.

Michael-De-La-Noy, 4 Denton Court.

N

Neil Joblin, c/o Casualty Department, Royal Hospital.

Knut Johansen, Norsk Rikskringkasting,
BERGEN, Norway.

O

Oggy Clarke - ?

P

ADDRESSES

Q

Queen Elizabeth, Buckingham Palace, Buckingham
Palace Road, London.

R

Rizakyzz Wzyzzamzzy, 9 Kizzaki, Zwizzily, Poland.

S

Auntie Susan, Holloway Prison, London.
Grandma Sugden, 10 Dolt Pastures, Norfolk.
Sean (B.A.Hons) Oxbridge Road.

Simon Shatzburger, 147 Star Close, Nottingham.

Geoff Strachan, (Editor of Community Magazine 11 New
Fetter Lane.

T

Dan Townsend, 21 Bob Marley Way, Mandela Park.

John Tydeman, (Adolescent Poetry) BBC, Portland Place.

ADDRESSES

U
Eunice Mole, Ward 9, Secure Unit, High Towers Hospital.

V
Auntie V (see under S)
Vicks, (future star in my opinion).

W
Wanker Williams, 69, Mulberry Bush Avenue.

Wilfred, c/o Careers Office. (If not there try dole office. If not there try pavements outside factorys and work places. Look for placard. it says 'Please give me a job'. Wilfred will be carrying it.)

XYZ
'X' Films, Dirty Franks Video Hire, 1, Pawn Way.
Yobby Dickson, Church Lads Brigade, Scout Hut.
Zenophobia Society, 47, England Packway.

NOTES

NOTES

ADRIAN MOLE MAN OF LETTERS

ONE OF THEM

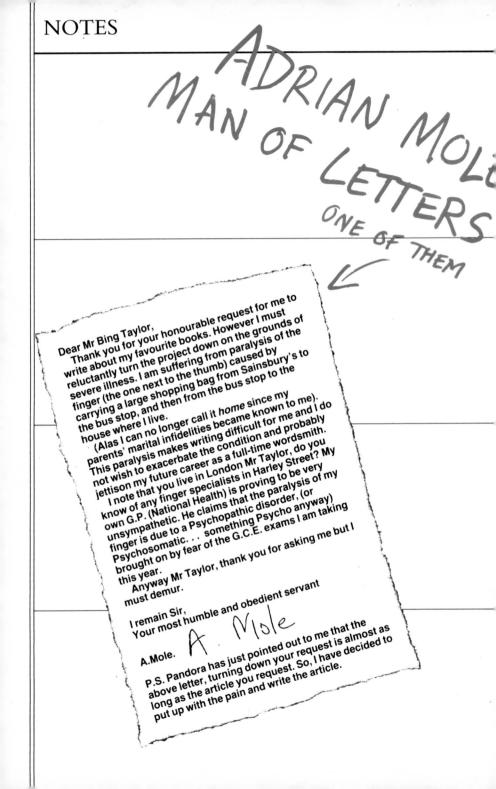

Dear Mr Bing Taylor,

Thank you for your honourable request for me to write about my favourite books. However I must reluctantly turn the project down on the grounds of severe illness. I am suffering from paralysis of the finger (the one next to the thumb) caused by carrying a large shopping bag from Sainsbury's to the bus stop, and then from the bus stop to the house where I live.

(Alas I can no longer call it *home* since my parents' marital infidelities became known to me). This paralysis makes writing difficult for me and I do not wish to exacerbate the condition and probably jettison my future career as a full-time wordsmith.

I note that you live in London Mr Taylor, do you know of any finger specialists in Harley Street? My own G.P. (National Health) is proving to be very unsympathetic. He claims that the paralysis of my finger is due to a Psychopathic disorder, (or Psychosomatic. . . something Psycho anyway) brought on by fear of the G.C.E. exams I am taking this year.

Anyway Mr Taylor, thank you for asking me but I must demur.

I remain Sir,
Your most humble and obedient servant

A.Mole.   A . Mole

P.S. Pandora has just pointed out to me that the above letter, turning down your request is almost as long as the article you request. So, I have decided to put up with the pain and write the article.

Braithwaite & Taylor

Braithwaite & Taylor Limited
91 Great Russell Street
London WC1V 3PS

Telephone
01-580 8466
01-637 2538 (Editorial)

THE GOOD BOOK GUIDE

Dear Mr. Mole,

The literary world is raving
about your erudition. As we pride
ourselves on being an independent
magazine devoted to promoting
literature available I am writing to select the best
would be willing to select your favourite books
for The Good Book Guide? would it you
I look forward eagerly to your response

Yours,

Brian Taylor

NOTES

The Diary of a Nobody George Grossmith and Weedon Grossmith I don't know why people laugh at poor Mr Pooter. He is a kind, respectable man. O.K. he is at odds with the world occasionally but is that any reason for the populace to snigger at his intimate jottings? I think George and Weedon Grossmith should be ashamed of themselves for finding and publishing his work.
Penguin p240 P
CMD022 £1.95

William Shakespeare: The Complete Works Edited by Peter Alexander I am trying to start a Shakespearean playreading society at school. We would meet during the dinner break; I am sick of standing around in the windy playground wasting my brain power. So far, only Pandora has joined, she wants our first reading to be Romeo and Juliet. But I want to do Hamlet which is a role perfectly suited to my introverted nature. We had a row in the cloakroom during which Pandora carried on like a shrew. I am no good at taming so she got her own way. Hopefully, our first meeting will take place in the Domestic Science room next Wednesday at 12.30, all welcome. We are doing Romeo and Juliet.
Collins p1408 P
CMB022 £4.95

NOTES

William the Bad Richmal Crompton William Brown and I have nothing in common. He is badly behaved, (indeed, he would be in the care of the Social Services if he lived today) and he still wears short trousers. Whereas, I am very well behaved (in fact almost a saint) and have been wearing Crimplene trousers for ages, (not the same pair).

Miss Richmal Crompton writes very well and is not afraid to use long difficult words. This book and the other William books force loud, undignified snorting and chortling laughter from me. Several times my parents have burst into my room thinking me to be in the middle of a severe fit, so unaccustomed are they to the sound of my laughter. I am not the sort of teenager who laughs easily; the world is a dead serious place. A word of advice from one who knows; the only William books that are worth reading, buying or borrowing are those that are illustrated by Thomas Henry.

Macmillan p272 [P]

CMC025 £1.50

NOTES

Pieces and Pontifications Norman Mailer Mr Mailer is clever *and* intellectual. The essays and short pieces in this book are a bit overpowering so only one or two should be read daily (before meals).

It is my opinion that Mr Mailer must have been under the influence of drink or New York at the time of writing this brilliant book.

It is just my luck to be a tee-totaller and living in a cul-de-sac.

Granada p192 Ⓟ   *CMC026 £3.95*

The Life and Loves of a She-Devil Fay Weldon I found this amongst the squalid mess on my mother's bedside table. It is all about how a very tall unattractive woman wreaks revenge on the husband who deserted her. By the end of the book the woman is medium height, rich and beautiful, and the husband is a gibbering penniless wreck.

I think my Father should read it before it is too late.

Coronet p240 Ⓟ   *CMC027 £1.95*

War and Peace Leo Tolstoy I don't know why people moan on about how long it takes to read this magnificent book, it only took me two days. All you have to do is to flick through it and skip all the boring descriptive passages. In fact even Tolstoy got fed up with describing *all* the battles. 'The Russian army, having retreated from Borodino, paused at Fili', is a good example of how he chickened out occasionally.

Penguin p145 Ⓟ   *CME967 £4.*

Scoop Evelyn Waugh This is a dead funny book about newspapers. It is especially interesting to me, because in between writing poems for a living when I'm grown up, I may, occasionally, dabble in a little light journalism. I wrote a fan letter to Ms Waugh last year (enclosing some of my poems) but alas she didn't reply.

CMD021 £1.95

Penguin p224 P

NOTES

NOTES

NOTES

NOTES

People don't know how difficult it is to act a tree. It
means that you must stand very still for nearly three
hours (unless there is a breeze and then you must sway
gently but without falling over). I had a few problems
with cherries dropping off my branches but apart from
that I was quite satisfied with my performance.

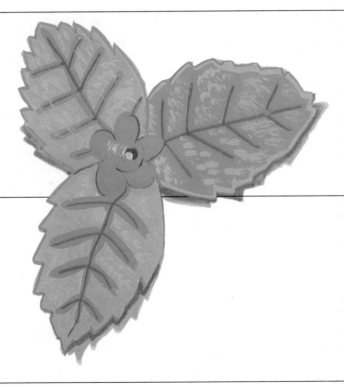

NOTES

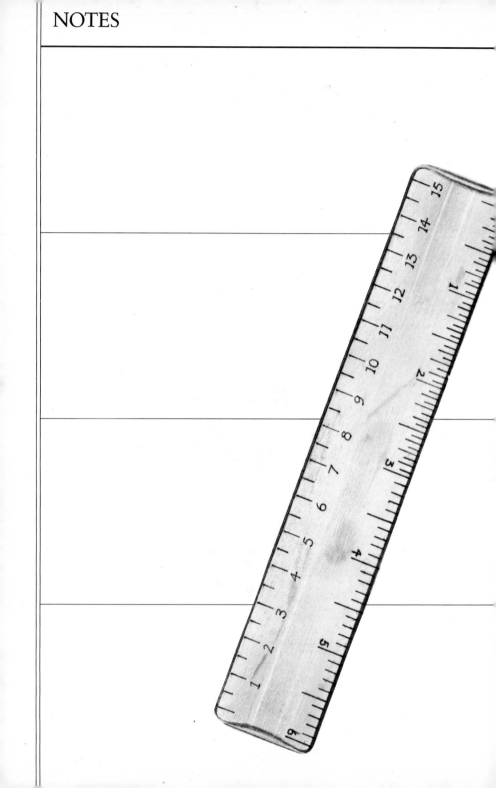